To my brother, Troy Armand, who explained to me the science of ice cream —G.A.

To my parents. Thanks for everything. —K.F.

To Pi —K.M.

Acknowledgments

Special thanks to Mary Jane Cary, Ice Screamers archive librarian,
and Eric Berley, The Franklin Fountain, Philadelphia

Authors' Note

This story is true to the known facts of Augustus Jackson's life and the realities of society during the time
he lived. However, in crafting this biography, we included some imagined scenes, people, and dialogue.
These parts of the story are dramatic extensions of historically documented events and interactions.

Text copyright © 2023 by Glenda Armand and Kim Freeman
Jacket art and interior illustrations copyright © 2023 by Keith Mallett

Visit us on the Web! rhcbooks.com

Educators and librarians, for a variety of teaching tools, visit us at RHTeachersLibrarians.com

Library of Congress Cataloging-in-Publication Data
Names: Armand, Glenda, author. | Freeman, Kim (Kimberly J.), author. | Mallett, Keith, illustrator.
Title: Ice cream man : how Augustus Jackson made a sweet treat better / by Glenda Armand and Kim Freeman ; illustrated by Keith Mallett.
Description: First edition. | New York : Crown Books for Young Readers, an imprint of Random House Children's Books, a division of Penguin Random House LLC, [2023] |
Includes bibliographical references. | Audience: Ages 3–7 | Audience: Grades K–1 |
Summary: "This picture book biography recounts the extraordinary life of Augustus Jackson, an African American entrepreneur who is known as the Father of Ice Cream." —Provided by publisher.
Identifiers: LCCN 2021061036 (print) | LCCN 2021061037 (ebook) | ISBN 978-0-593-56322-9 (trade) | ISBN 978-0-593-56323-6 (lib. bdg.) | ISBN 978-0-593-56324-3 (ebook)
Subjects: LCSH: Jackson, Augustus, 1808–1852—Juvenile literature. | Cooks—United States—Biography—Juvenile literature. |
African American cooks—Biography—Juvenile literature. | Ice cream, ices, etc.—History—Juvenile literature.
Classification: LCC TX649.J334 A76 2023 (print) | LCC TX649.J334 (ebook) | DDC 641.5092 [B]—dc23/eng/20220327

The artist used digital painting to create the illustrations for this book.
The text of this book is set in 16-point Winchester New ITC.
Interior design by Elizabeth Tardiff

MANUFACTURED IN CHINA
10 9 8 7 6 5 4 3
First Edition

Random House Children's Books supports the First Amendment and celebrates the right to read.

Ice Cream Man

How Augustus Jackson Made a Sweet Treat Better

by Glenda Armand and Kim Freeman

illustrated by Keith Mallett

Crown Books for Young Readers

New York

On a hot summer day in 1850, Augustus Jackson's familiar voice could be heard from a block away as he strolled down Philadelphia's cobblestone streets.

He pushed his cart and sang his familiar tune:

"It's hot, hot, hot! Come on 'n' cool down!
Ol' Gus has the greatest ice cream in town!
Got lotsa flavors, so take your pick!
Step right up and have a lick!"

"Ice Cream Man!" children shouted as they came running. "Ice Cream Man!"
Augustus Jackson stopped and greeted them with a smile. *That's right,*
he thought. *I am the Ice Cream Man.* For him, it was a dream come true.

The children gathered around the cart. Each, in turn, handed a penny to the Ice Cream Man.

He spooned out his sweet treat and remembered how his dream began.

Augustus Jackson was born in 1808 in Philadelphia, Pennsylvania. At that time, most African Americans were enslaved—forced to work under cruel conditions for no pay. But in Pennsylvania, slavery was against the law. So while Augustus and his family were free, they were also poor. They worked together in their garden and raised chickens for food.

Augustus enjoyed helping his mother cook for his brothers and sisters. Soon he prepared entire meals. His family praised his skills.

"Why, Gus, you could cook for pay!"

Could I? Gus wondered. *Could this be a way to help my family?* He began to dream of becoming a professional cook.

One day, when he was only twelve years old, Gus decided to follow his dream.

Gus said goodbye to his mother, brothers, and sisters and hitched a ride with family friends who were on their way to Washington, DC. They knew of a place that could use Gus's cooking skills.

When Gus arrived, he did not waste any time. He applied for a job at the White House.

Gus met Jennie Trigger, the head cook. He learned that even though she was enslaved, Jennie ran the kitchen.

Jennie took a liking to Gus and hired him to be a kitchen helper.

"Work hard," Jennie told him, "and I'll make you a cook."

"Yes, ma'am!" said Gus, and he started work the next day.

Gus milked the White House dairy cows.

He tended the garden.

He rotated meats over the fire in
the kitchen fireplace.

At night, he slept in a room for both free and enslaved servants.

Five years later, seventeen-year-old Gus had a new job. He was a cook! His dream had come true.

Gus became an expert at making a cold, sweet pudding with eggs and milk. It was called ice cream, and it had been a favorite of presidents since George Washington. Gus made the sweet treat in an ice cream "machine"—a wooden bucket with a metal canister inside.

Making ice cream was a slow process. Gus had to time it just right so it would be ready when dessert was served.

The delicacy brought smiles to the faces of the rich, important White House guests. Their smiles grew even wider when Gus created a new, lighter mixture without eggs.

One day, while preparing a special dinner, Gus asked Jennie, "Why should only the fancy-dressed people enjoy ice cream? Why not make everyone smile?"

Now Gus had a new dream: He would make ice cream for everyone!

At the age of twenty-two, Gus said goodbye to Jennie and his friends at the

White House and returned to his hometown to embark on his next adventure.

Back in Philadelphia, Gus opened his very own ice cream parlor.

In the White House, the guests ate Gus's delicious delicacy right away.
Now that he had a shop, he had to make his ice cream last longer. So he spooned
it into quart-sized tins and placed the tins in buckets filled with chipped ice.
Then he set the buckets on a big block of ice.

Customers crowded inside the parlor to try Gus's one-of-a-kind ice cream flavors.

Sometimes Gus brought the ice cream to the customers.
He pushed his cart down Goodwater Street, chanting merrily:

"Ice cream! Ice cream! Come and taste!
Get it 'fore it melts! No time to waste!
Strawberry, mint, and vanilla, too!
Step right up! Try something new!"

Gus sold all the ice cream he could make!

Gus's success inspired other people to open ice cream parlors, too. But no one could make ice cream as frosty, smooth, and sweet as he could. So Gus had an idea. Why not sell his ice cream to the new shop owners?

He would do just that! But he would have to invent a way to make his ice cream faster. And he had to make it last even longer.

One day, Gus made his ice cream the same way he always did. He poured the ingredients—sugar, cream, and one of his tasty flavorings—into the ice cream machine's metal canister. Then he took the lid, which had a paddle attached to the inside, and tightened it onto the canister.

Gus placed the canister inside the wooden bucket. Next, he filled the space around the canister with ice.

But on this day in 1832, he added something to the ice—ROCK SALT!

Then he twisted the canister's handle. Back and forth, swish, swish! The paddle whipped and spun the mixture.

Soon Gus removed the lid. Inside was his famous ice cream! He had made it in half the time!

Gus had discovered that rock salt made the mixture freeze more quickly.

And the sooner it froze, the faster it became Gus's great-tasting ice cream.

So he made more and more, and he created new flavors.

Back and forth: Rum raisin!

Back and forth: Butter pecan!

Swish, swish: Chocolate!

Now Gus could make enough ice cream for the new shop owners and his regular customers, too!

The shop owners paid the enormous sum of $1 a quart. But it was worth every penny!

Folks in Philly ate it up!

Another one of Gus's dreams came true when his whole family came to work in his parlor. They packed his ice cream in rock salt and ice, and they sold it near and far. They shipped it by train to New York City, which was one hundred miles away. And it didn't melt!

Gus's thoughts came back to the present.

He finished spooning out the ice cream to his eager customers.

He had realized his dream and more. But even better, Augustus Jackson made people smile.

Philly's original Ice Cream Man continued on his way, singing:

"Ice cream! Ice cream! Quite a treat!

Come smile awhile and beat the heat!

Try butter pecan—rum raisin, too!

Got a sweet tooth? Made just for you!"

And still today, who can eat ice cream without smiling?

Make Your Own Ice Cream

You will need:

1 gallon-sized zip-top plastic bag

1 quart-sized zip-top plastic bag

1 bag of ice

½ cup of half-and-half

1 tablespoon of sugar

½ teaspoon of vanilla

2 tablespoons of your favorite flavoring: chocolate syrup, strawberries, peanut butter—whatever you like

⅓ cup of rock salt

Instructions:

1. Fill the gallon-sized bag halfway with ice.
2. Fill the quart-sized bag with the half-and-half, sugar, vanilla, and your flavoring. Smoosh the bag to combine the ingredients. Zip the bag closed, removing as much air as possible.
3. Add rock salt into the large bag with ice.
4. Place the smaller bag with the liquid inside the larger bag and remove as much air as possible before zipping it closed.
5. Shake or toss the bag for five to ten minutes until the ice cream forms.
6. Remove the smaller bag from the larger bag and squeeze the ice cream into a bowl. Or place the smaller bag in the freezer to eat later.

Enjoy!

Afterword

Augustus Jackson led a remarkable life for an African American who lived between the American Revolution and the Civil War. He was born free on April 16, 1808. Very little is known about his childhood or personal life. We do know that when Jackson was only twelve years old, he left Philadelphia for Washington, DC.

He became a cook in the White House and served presidents James Monroe, John Quincy Adams, and Andrew Jackson.

Jackson discovered that an egg-based custard called ice cream was a dessert served frequently at the White House. The dish was prepared with flavors that most people now would consider strange and unappetizing in ice cream: Parmesan cheese, asparagus, and oyster! Jackson became an expert at making the dish. Soon he created an eggless version. This is what we know today as ice cream.

After he left the White House, Jackson devoted the rest of his life to making, selling, and improving ice cream. Before he made his contribution to confectionery, ice cream had been enjoyed almost exclusively by the wealthy in private settings.

When Jackson opened his ice cream parlor and catering business in 1830, he devised a way to keep the ice cream frozen so that it could be shipped and sold to other businesses. Since freezers had not yet been invented, Jackson spooned the ice cream into tin cans and stored the tin cans in buckets of ice that were then placed on a block of ice.

In 1832, Jackson pioneered the practice of adding rock salt to the ice used in making ice cream. This innovation sped up production, allowing him to make more ice cream and sell it to more people. There is no record of Jackson ever obtaining a patent for his creations.

Nevertheless, Jackson is often referred to as "the man who invented ice cream" or "the father of ice cream." In fact, the first form of ice cream was invented in China around 200 BCE when a milk and rice mixture was frozen by packing it into snow.

So while Jackson did not invent ice cream, he did help perfect the process of manufacturing it by coming up with the idea of using rock salt, which is still used to make ice cream today. His business made him one of the wealthiest African Americans in Philadelphia. The price of the $1-a-quart tins of ice cream he sold would be equivalent to $27 a quart today.

Jackson is reported to have died in a train accident on January 11, 1852. His daughter and relatives continued to run his business for a few years after his death. His ice cream parlor may be long gone, but the sweet legacy of Augustus Jackson, the Ice Cream Man, will live forever.

Sources

Coard, Michael. "Black Geniuses You May or May Not Know About." *The Philadelphia Tribune*, September 18, 2015. phillytrib.com/commentary /black-geniuses-you-may-or-may-not-know-about/article_a3d6ce6b-e209-5d81-a576-4d2bcb6c550d.html.

"History of Ice Cream." *In Mama's Kitchen*, November 26, 2019. inmamaskitchen.com/history-of-food/history-of-ice-cream.

"Ice Cream à la 1800s." *Damsels in Regress*, July 4, 2010. damselsinregress.wordpress.com/2010/07/04/ice-cream-a-la-1800s.

"Ice Cream First Made by Negro Caterer." *Atoka County Gazette*, July 27, 1928.

Miller, Adrian. *The President's Kitchen Cabinet: The Story of the African Americans Who Have Fed Our First Families, from the Washingtons to the Obamas.* Chapel Hill: The University of North Carolina Press, 2017.

Montoya, Carolina. "Augustus Jackson." Prezi, March 1, 2014. prezi.com/aiq_h90bhojl/Augustus-Jackson.

Mosley, Derek. "The 'Father of Ice Cream' You May Not Know." *On Milwaukee*, February 27, 2020. onmilwaukee.com/articles/the-father-of-ice -cream-black-history.

"Philadelphia Ice Cream." *The United States Gazette*, July 18, 1838.

Smith, Starex. "Lauderhill's Newest Ice Cream Parlor Got That Work! #Delicious." *The Hungry Black Man*, October 5, 2018. thehungryblackman .com/2018/10/05/lauderhills-newest-ice-cream-parlor-got-that-work-delicious/.

Tesauro, Michael. "Ruminations: A Brief History of Ice Cream." *Life & Thyme*, September 1, 2016. lifeandthyme.com/food/reflections/ruminations -brief-history-ice-cream.

"The Origin of Ice Cream." *The New York Times*, March 11, 1894.

"The Real Scoop on Ice Cream's History." Gold Coast Ice Cream, August 1, 2019. goldcoasticecream.com/the-real-scoop-on-ice-creams-history/.

Walton, Lester. "Philly Citizen Was First Maker of Ice Cream." *The Pittsburgh Courier*, May 19, 1928.

Wilkes, Leigh Ann. "How to Make Ice Cream in a Bag." *Leigh Anne Wilkes*, June 23, 2018. yourhomebasedmom.com/ice-cream-bag/.

Yun, Molly. "Ice Cream: An American Favorite Since the Founding Fathers." PBS. pbs.org/food/features/ice-cream-founding-fathers.